Amelia Earhart was born July 24, 1897 in Atchison, Kansas, the older daughter of [...] Earhart, a minister's son and a graduate of Theil College o[...] School, and his wife, Amy Otis, daughter of a United State[...] Amelia's birth came that of her sister Muriel, from whose b[...] Price, the text of this book has been excerpted.

We grew up in Kansas City, Kansas. In 1904, when Dad [...] [le]gal work for a railroad, he took us to see the World's Fair in Saint Louis. Amelia and Dad rode on an elephant, and on the Ferris wheel, but that fascinating new invention, the roller coaster, was thought too dangerous. When we got home, we decided to build our own roller coaster with the aid of our neighboring playmate, Ralphie Martin.

Amelia decided that our back yard tool-shed, which stood about eight feet high, would be the starting point for our coaster, so we pulled several long two-by-fours through the cellar window and put them up against the shed roof. By means of the kitchen stepladder we got to the ridgepole, but we were stymied when we attempted to anchor our boards there. We resolved to seek adult aid in the person of our young Uncle Carl. Conspiratorially we seized upon him as he came up the front sidewalk that evening and led him to the back yard where Amelia explained our difficulties. His reaction was practical and satisfactorily non-adult. He said, "You need some long, long nails to fix the slide to the roof. You better nail your track together with boards, like ties, you know. I'll bring some big nails home tomorrow."

All the next day Amelia, Ralphie, and I hammered and sawed. We found a wooden packing box, and taking one side which was about fourteen inches square, we nailed two parallel boards on the underside about three inches apart to grip the single track. We soon realized that the pitch would be too great if we used only one fourteen-foot section of "track," so we made a support about one foot high, which Ralph, with his superior vocabulary, said was a "trestle." This reduced the angle considerably and, as Amelia said, it would give us a longer ride, too. Uncle Carl, whom Amelia and I called "Nicey" for obvious reasons, brought the long nails, which he obligingly pounded into a stud on the roof. He gave some sturdy blows to our rather shaky trestle and said, "Fine! Hook it up now and get some grease on the track and you'll have a coaster almost as good as the one at Electric Park!"

At dinner that evening questions about the pounding behind the shed were parried by his nonchalant reply, "Oh, they're just making a play railroad out there!"

This remark was accompanied by an obvious wink at Amelia which sent us into such spasms of giggles that Mother threatened to send us from the table without dessert.

The next morning we took a half pail of lard from the icebox and greased the track. We hooked the two lengths of track together and the little car, empty, was pushed off on its trial run. We had neglected to provide any kind of a launching platform, but we were all too eager to have a ride to bother with such an unnecessary appurtenance. Amelia held on to the edge of the roof while I held the car from the ladder, as she got on the car with her legs doubled against her chest.

"Let me go!" she shrieked, and I did.

#2813

Amelia's first "flight" —the "rolly coaster."

Zoom! she went down the track. There was a sound of splintering wood and a crash as the car and its passenger left the track when the car hit the trestle and tipped it over. Amelia jumped up, her eyes alight, ignoring a torn stocking and bruised lip as she exclaimed happily, "Oh, Pidge, it's just like flying!" Then, ever practical, she added, "We must build more track and a stronger trestle!"

This was unfortunately not to be, for the sound of the splintering boards brought Mother running from the house, as well as our next door neighbor. "Why, that's terribly dangerous," Mother said, looking up at the shed roof. "You might break an arm or leg if you fell off, eight feet from the ground! It must come down at once!"

"But, Mother, we'll fix it stronger. Please let it stay—we worked so hard to build it!" pleaded Amelia, while I sat down and cried without restraint.

I still believe that if Mother had waited until Dad came home to ask him, we should have been allowed to keep our coaster, as he was in favor of our being as much like boys as we wanted. However, our track was soon pulled down, and Sadie dragged the boards back to the cellar.

To compensate for the loss of our coaster, Mother and Dad got us a lawn swing—a wooden contraption with two seats facing each other suspended from a high frame. It was meant for gentle family swinging, Mother explained, but soon we discovered that it did not have to swing gently all the time. By standing back to back with our hands on the suspending bars, we could get up a momentum that made the whole frame sway and jump. We found it was exciting to swing with knees hooked over the upright bar and heads hanging down, instead of demurely seated.

Another satisfactory means of channeling off surplus energy was devised by Uncle Nicey, who built us a "flying Dutchman" after obtaining grudging parental permission. A flying Dutchman, for any who are not familiar with that noble means of entertainment, is the primal leg-propelled merry-go-round. A long heavy board, twelve feet or so in length, is fastened by a single spike to a stump or a solidly planted log about four feet high; the spike must be loose enough so that the board revolves easily. We used to run madly, Amelia pushing on one end and I on the other until we had worked up momentum; then we both jumped on the board and whirled around until "she died."

It was this thoroughly delightful, tomboyish activity which led to our emancipation from skirts. Mother was really quite "advanced" in having a sewing woman make us "gym suits" for play, since all nice little girls at the turn of the century wore long full-skirted dresses with ruffled pinafores over them. Mother had two suits of dark blue flannel made for us with generous pleated bloomers gathered at the knees. We were comfortable, unconventional, and entirely happy tomboys, thanks to a forward-looking mother who endured the neighbors' raised eyebrows with equanimity.

Books and animals were always important in our lives. We could repeat *Peter Rabbit* word for word long before we could read, although both of us read before we were five.

"The first place I well remember was a large pleasant meadow with a pond of cool water in it"—the opening line of *Black Beauty* is still fresh in my memory. Anna Sewell's great story about a horse made an indelible impression on Amelia and me, aroused a crusading spirit, and deepened the affection with which we regarded all four-footed creatures. We lived at a time when "stylish turnouts" meant horses tortured by check-reins, bobbed tails, and cruel bits; when "grocery boys" lashed half-starved animals up and down the streets delivering "telephone orders"; when tired milk-wagon horses were forced to race to the stables after having been driven on a milk route since four o'clock in the morning. Amelia and I read and re-read the tale

The "Flying Dutchman," a favorite game.

of the sufferings of Beauty and Ginger and were fired with anger against cruel adults. With Amelia, to feel something deeply was to take action about it. We began with our next-door neighbor, Mr. Oldham.

Mr. Oldham had a beautiful little mare, Nellie, whom he stabled in a small low-roofed shed in his back yard. Soon after he acquired her, Nellie, driven frantic by the flies and the terrific Kansas summer heat, kicked and neighed in torment. Amelia begged Dad to lead Nellie out of the shed and let her graze awhile in our yard. Dad, a humane and gentle person, overcame his repugnance to interfere unasked in a neighbor's affairs and was as righteously indignant at the poor creature's treatment as we were. He urged Mr. Oldham to build a proper barn and screen it. "If you don't, you are likely to have a complaint for creating a public nuisance," Dad told him one stifling evening.

The summer wore on and Mr. Oldham did nothing about a barn, but tried to break Nellie's spirit by whipping her around the legs when she kicked in her vile, cramped stall. Amelia and I constituted ourselves a "Help Nellie" brigade. Whenever we heard the first restless kicks, we would dash to the shed, and climbing on the box we planted by the tiny window, we would reach in to pat the glossy, sweating neck and give her a little handful of grass and clover, to try to calm her, so she would not be punished.

One day, as Mr. Oldham was unharnessing her outside the shed, a piece of newspaper blew across the yard, and she reared in fright. Instead of gentling her, he seized the whip from the carriage and gave her a vicious cut. In fright and frenzy, Nellie jumped forward and pulled the loosely tied hitching rein free. Then she galloped down the driveway with traces and reins flying and with Mr. Oldham shouting and swearing in pursuit. At the foot of the hill there was a wayward branch of the Kaw River—sometimes a roaring torrent, as at this time of year, but more often a mere trickle of water spanned by a narrow bridge. The cry of "Runaway! Runaway!" brought people running from their houses, and a few volunteer cowboys hurried over to the bridge, hoping to turn the frenzied creature back up the hill where her capture would be easy. Desperation drove the little mare to swerve from the waiting posse. She jumped over the wooden railing, plunging to her death in the water below.

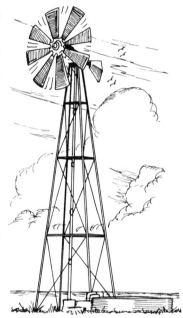

Mr. Oldham had turned his ankle and bruised himself in his race after Nellie, so he was confined to his home for several days. In the tradition of neighborliness, Mother planned to send over a generous piece of the cake Sadie had just made.

"Amelia," she called. "I want you to take this cake over to Mr. Oldham and ask how he is feeling."

Amelia came and stood before Mother. She put her hands behind her back and soberly shook her head. Mother looked in amazement at the small rebel, for such insubordination was unknown in our family.

"Mother," said Amelia, "I won't take cake or anything to that horrid man. After the way he treated Nellie, I'm glad he got hurt! Spank me if you want to; I just won't do it."

Mother felt more or less the same way, I am sure, and recognizing a martyr to principle, she said no more about Amelia's refusal to make the friendly gesture. Later, after Sadie had returned from the errand, she told Mother that we would not have to worry about Mr. Oldham's keeping another horse in the shed: "He's bound ter git one o' dem horseless kerridges, Mis' Oldham says. He figgers they'll be a heap safer!"

Amelia fishing with her father.

Years afterward, Amelia came across the poem by Vachel Lindsay, "The Bronco That Wouldn't Be Broken of Dancing." She showed it to me and said, "Nellie!" I nodded.

In Atchison we were never far from the country. Our father sometimes took us fishing, or our Mother took us on picnics with our beloved Challis cousins. Holidays and birthdays were always times for family celebrations, and Amelia's birthday, coming at the height of midsummer, was usually marked by a picnic or a garden party with cake and homemade ice cream, which all the family helped produce by taking a turn at "grinding the freezer." Licking the ice cream off the dasher was as much a part of the festivities as blowing out the candles on the cake. I think, however, we liked the picnics best, because we could run wild through the woods with no worries about soiling or mussing fussy party dresses. Under Mother's intelligent direction we became ardent amateur entomologists at an early age. She never said, "Oh, a horrid worm!" or, "Ugh, a spider—sweep it out quick!" but, "Come, girls, let's look at old Mr. Worm and find out how he gets around so well," or, "See what a wonderful lacy home Mrs. Spider makes." We had a special box with a screen on top, and there we kept our specimens after we had identified them in Amelia's copy of *Insect Life*.

In those days chickens were bought "on the hoof." After Sadie had decapitated the Sunday fowl, she plunged the still twitching body into a pail of boiling water and plucked the feathers out by the handful. She then brought the chicken into the kitchen where Mother cleaned it and cut it up. We were always an interested audience when Mother performed this operation because the wonder of God's creation, not the messiness of the task, was stressed.

"See, girls," she would say, "how neatly this hen's little lungs fit here, just above her tiny heart." Or, "See how the wings are jointed—just like our wrists and elbows."

After one of our all-day outings in the late summer we brought back a graceful pale green Luna moth and a Pandorus who was depositing her eggs and beating her gay wings to shreds to perpetuate the species, according to Nature's law. We had some goggle-eyed katydids and a tree toad living peaceably with a praying mantis. One day Uncle Carl had brought home a tiny chameleon which he bought from a circus vendor as a surprise donation to his nieces' "Bug Party," as he jokingly christened our museum. He had told us that the salesman assured him the chameleon would want nothing to eat for three days; then a dozen freshly killed flies would make him happy for another three-day period. We stopped to look at the Pandorus, but we were greeted by a shocking sight: the Pandorus, the Luna, and the katydids were no more—only a well-fed and sleepy chameleon was basking greenly in the sun at the front of the cage.

"Oh, you bad old chameleon! You've eaten our beautiful Luna and Pandorus!" wailed Amelia when she discovered the cannibalism.

Mother, just and practical, assuaged our grief somewhat by saying, "No, Amelia, you girls must not blame the chameleon. He was simply doing what Mother Nature told him to do. He was hungry, so he went hunting for his breakfast. It's just like the fox that steals Grandfather's chickens once in a while. It's only people who know it's wrong to take other people's things."

Our father's work as a railroad claims lawyer took our family to Des Moines, Iowa. Mother distrusted the public schools there at first, and imported Mrs. Gardiner, a young widow, to act as our tutor. She disapproved of Dad's encouraging us in our tomboyish ways and she spoke out angrily against Dad's "undermining influence" when he brought us a football instead of sewing baskets for a Thanksgiving gift. Her presence at mealtimes was a continual damper upon Dad's humor. She was shocked when he said one day to Mother, "Well, old girl, I'll have to get you a better saw so you can saw up that cordwood in the back yard!" We children knew this to be the baldest kind of irony and we chuckled delightedly when Mother caught the ball and replied, meekly, "Oh, Edwin, that will be so nice. I did have a hard time with those last logs!" Mrs. Gardiner did not return from her Christmas holiday, and we entered the public school, Amelia in seventh grade and I in the fourth.

When Dad was promoted to be head of the Claims Department, he was able for the first

The highlight of the picnic was the sending off of two hot air balloons which Dad bought from Des Moines.

time in his married life to take a vacation, and we spent the month of August in Worthington, Minnesota, on the shores of a small lake, Okabena, with fishing, boating, and swimming. We stayed at the home of the local postmaster, Mr. J. P. Mann, who treated us like members of the family, and his daughters Grace and Genevieve were our playmates.

Genevieve's sixteenth birthday, August twenty-first, was celebrated by a picnic at a lake about twenty miles from Worthington. We were going to make the journey in two "touring cars," a Reo and a Stoddard Dayton. This was the first time that any of our family had been in an automobile although we had seen a few on the streets of Des Moines. We covered the twenty miles in less than two hours because the roads were packed hard and we had no tire "punctures."

Second to the drive in the automobile, the highlight of the picnic was the sending off of two hot air balloons which Dad had brought from Des Moines. One was shaped like a teardrop about six feet high, and the other was an elephant eight feet long and nearly that high. These balloons were made of heavy tissue paper fastened to a light bamboo hoop about twelve inches in diameter. Secured in the center of this hoop by wires was a fist-sized pack of excelsior impregnated with kerosene, which heated the air inside the balloon and caused it to ascend. It seems incredible to me now that people were permitted to release these balloons, which constituted such a fire hazard, for a gust of wind could cause the balloon to tip and catch fire from the burning pack which, still glowing, would, of course, fall to earth. In theory they stayed aloft until the pack burned out and with the hot air inside cooling, the balloon floated harmlessly down. Dad directed holding the balloon while he lighted the fuel pack on a large flat rock on the lake shore. We gathered around the red, white and blue teardrop, gently pulling the paper sides away from the flame, and holding to it with thumb and forefinger. As soon as the air inside the balloon became heated, it began to pull upward. We held it down until the hot air made the paper stretch so that there was nothing to grasp. Then Dad said, "All right! Let her go!" and it slipped from our hands and went soaring over the lake, higher and higher, until it was just a tiny spark in the evening sky.

The elephant was a great success because Nicey had attached to the hoop a large cardboard sign which read, "Happy Birthday, Gen" for the elephant to carry aloft. Watching him disappear over the trees, we sang "Auld Lang Syne." We then hurried to get into the automobiles for the return trip, as both drivers wanted to be home before dark, since the carriage lamps did not give much light on the road, and as Dad remarked, "An engine still hasn't got the sense a horse has about a hole in the road."

In the cow pasture across the road from the Mann's home, there were several piles of whitened bones which Genevieve told us were the skeletons of three cows that had perished in a blizzard three years before. Amelia wanted to put together a complete skeleton on the ground, but with only the living cows grazing near as models, it was hard to place many of the small bones. We spent hours trying to number and arrange in order the vertebrae and tail bones of any one of the cows. The ribs were a puzzle, too, as we could not count the ribs on the live cows because they were too well fed. Her research won Amelia the nickname of Dr. Bones with the Worthington people, but as Mother vetoed our plan of bringing a bushel basketful of bones back to Des Moines for further study in our cellar, the interest died, and the nickname, too.

This happy summer was unfortunately a prelude to a period which saw the loss of our material prosperity and the beginning of the disintegration of our family. I find it difficult to write of the deterioration of Dad's character and yet I know that the hardship and mental suffering that Amelia and I endured as adolescents made an indelible impression upon us and help to explain some of Amelia's actions and attitudes in her later life. Now that Dad was successful, he had the money to enjoy sociability after work with friends at the hotel bar. They were used to social drinking, he was not, and he could not hold his liquor as they did. He began to make mistakes at work, and we treated him with cold scorn at home. At eleven and thirteen years of age we could not know the psychological roots of Dad's behavior; we only knew that

In the cow pasture across the road from the Mann's house there were several piles of whitened bones.

he did not seem to care at all for us any more and that we had lost our adored companionable Dad.

Dad lost his responsible job, and got a lesser one in St. Paul, Minnesota. We were strangers there in high school, and only beginning to make friends when we moved again. This time Dad worked in Springfield, Missouri, while Mother, Amelia and I stayed in Chicago with friends. I entered the small Morgan Park High School. Amelia, however, after interviewing the principal, declined to go there as she said the chemistry laboratory was "a kitchen sink." She set out to visit several of the high schools which were within commuting distance, and she asked just one question of the principals: "May I please see your chemistry laboratory?" She chose Hyde Park High School.

The years immediately preceding and during World War I were notable for outrageous municipal graft in Chicago. Although we were not affected directly by most of the corruption, even the school system was used as a place where political influence could get one a job without competence. It was a shock for Amelia and me to face teachers who could not teach. Amelia was assigned to a senior English class with a Miss Dingee, who, it was rumored, was an aunt of the mayor's wife. So deaf that she could not hear her students, Miss Dingee always told them to read quietly, and spent the period reading a book herself. The students mocked her, but she could not hear them.

Amelia prepared a petition asking that Miss Dingee be replaced by a teacher "who can teach us something." The two girls who had helped her prepare it refused to sign, for their parents feared City Hall's reaction. Amelia spoke to the class above the laughing and talking. "Will you please listen a minute? I think it's a shame the way we've been treating poor Miss Dingee. She can't help it if she can't hear, but just the same we ought to have a teacher who will teach us something, and I think we ought to ask the principal to give us a different teacher. Will you sign this petition?" A clamor of opposition broke out, and the petition was seized and torn into little pieces and scattered in the aisles. Amelia persuaded the school librarian to let her read in the library instead of in Miss Dingee's class and thus she earned the sobriquet of "The girl in brown who walks alone," as the yearbook called her.

After a year in Chicago, we rejoined Dad in Kansas City, where he was practicing law. Mother now received her inheritance from her parents, and was able to send Amelia to Ogontz School in Rydal, Pennsylvania, to prepare for college. Amelia was invited to join one of the three secret societies at the school. Here she enjoyed the carefully guarded ritual and the camaraderie of the members until she found that there were some girls at Ogontz who did not belong to any sorority. She urged her own group to take in more girls, but this idea was not accepted. Then she went to the headmistress, and asked that the faculty approve four secret societies instead of three. She declared, "Every girl ought to have the fun of belonging to a

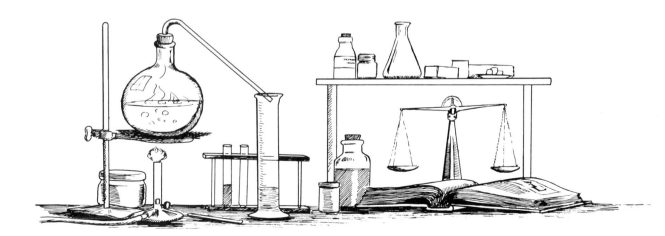

Amelia at the Spadina Military Hospital as a voluntary aid.

sorority if she wants to." I do not know the outcome of this crusade of Amelia's, but I imagine her concern came from the days at Hyde Park when she, too, had been an outsider.

Amelia maintained that girls should not only be free to join or not to join sororities, but that they should also be free mentally to explore through discussion and reading any topic under the sun. She rebelled specifically when in the class reading Ibsen's plays, attention was centered solely upon the problem of the over-protected wife in *A Doll's House. Ghosts*, in which attention is focused upon venereal disease, and *Hedda Gabler*, which deals with suicidal insanity, were tabu.

During the spring of Amelia's first year at Ogontz, the United States entered World War I. I believe it was because of her feeling that women traditionally were relegated to a secondary position in the conduct of war that she began her scrapbook on women's careers. She cut from magazines and newspapers items telling of the achievements of women in fields usually considered man's domain. Among the yellowed clippings in the small notebook, I find ones dealing with a woman forest service fire lookout, a woman doctor, a Bombay woman lawyer, a Toronto woman bricklayer, a woman bellringer, a woman bank president, and others.

I was studying at St. Margaret's College in Toronto. When Amelia came to spend Christmas holidays with me, she was shocked by the number of injured soldiers, who had been sent home to recover from wounds received in the fighting in France. Seeing a chance to do something more useful than studying, Amelia decided not to return to Ogontz. She took an intensive course in Red Cross First Aid, and enrolled in the Voluntary Aid Detachment, which sent her to the Spadina Military Hospital.

Her knowledge of chemistry impressed the Director of Nurses, and she was soon promoted to the diet kitchen. Amelia felt that hospital life was dreary enough without having drab and unappetizing meals, if it was possible to improve them. One day she approached the head dietician, a formidable Englishwoman named Mrs. Waldron. Amelia asked to have stewed tomatoes alternated with the turnip and parsnips which were served as a second vegetable with military regularity. She had figures to show that the cost of tomatoes would be less than a cent more per serving and, aside from a few non-acid diets, they could be served to all the patients who now were having the parsnips and turnips. She ended her plea, "And, Mrs. Waldron, tomatoes are so much cheerfuller." The next supply order contained fifty large cans of tomatoes.

One minor skirmish was won; now on to another, this time against rice pudding. Some of the long-term men used to groan when they saw it on the trays, and she was often greeted by plaintive remarks. Two men whose beds were adjoining emptied out their rice pudding on the tray one day and, covering a spoon with it, heaped the pudding into a grave-like mound which they marked with matches bent to form letters "R.I.P."

Amelia, without identifying the "Rest in Peace" artists, again appealed to Mrs. Waldron for a variation. "Blanc mange is just as nourishing and a little strawberry or cherry flavoring will make it tasty and colorful. I'll stay to make it up the night before, so it will harden in time for dinner."

When the extra milk, cornstarch, and flavoring were delivered, Amelia had the help of the whole staff in making the first batch. One girl brought some fancy molds from home; another contributed some candied cherries and orange slices, which owing to wartime rationing were highly prized confections. The word somehow "got around" the wards that the American sister was responsible for making this "sweet" to replace the rice puddings. The two matchstick artists outdid themselves by printing this message on a noticeably cleared tray:

"RAY, RAY,

U.S.A.!"

When Amelia's day off coincided with my free Saturday from St. Margaret's we allowed ourselves the extravagance of horseback riding. One Saturday morning, upon entering the stables, we noticed a big rawboned dappled gray that we had not seen before. Amelia said to March, the groom, "I'd like to ride that big fellow sometime, March, unless he's privately owned."

Amelia's father took her to watch some Jennies flying.

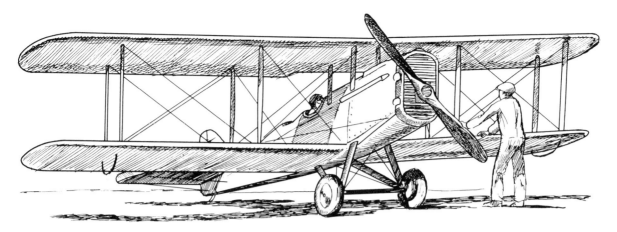

"Well, Miss," March replied, "It don't look like nobody's going to ride that old devil. His name's Dynamite, and he used to belong to an old-time cavalry colonel, and I figure he got pretty mean treatment, because he sure is like a stick of dynamite now. He tossed off two of the boys who tried to ride him yesterday, and he lashed out with his hoofs, so it's a wonder he didn't kill them both. No, Miss, I don't think you better try him."

Amelia divided the apple she had brought for the horse she was riding that day, and stepped over to Dynamite's stall. As soon as he heard a step beside him, back went his ears close to his head, and with bared teeth he said plainly he wanted no part of the human race. Amelia just clucked softly to him and put the piece of apple in his feed box; then she patted his neck lightly and slipped out of the stall. As we rode out of the stable, Amelia said, "I'm going to ask March to let me stop in for a few minutes every afternoon on the way home from the hospital to try to tame that poor Dynamite."

Little by little her kindness and courage won him, and within a month's time, he had come to accept a brisk canter with an easy bit and a light-handed rider as decidedly preferable to staging a one-horse rebellion because of ancient wrongs. The owner of the stables would never accept a fee when Amelia rode Dynamite because he said she had saved the horse for him by making him a useful member of the animal working force again instead of an outlaw.

One of the officers who rode with us several times was an officer in the Royal Flying Corps. He admired the way in which Amelia managed Dynamite and one day he said, "Miss Earhart, watching you ride that big, ugly horse reminds me of the way I have to fly my plane. Sometimes she goes along smooth as silk and then she gets contrary and bucks a bit just to show off, like Dynamite does. I'd like to invite you and your sister to come out to the airfield at Armor Heights next week and watch us ride *our* nags."

Amelia knew a number of pilots who were patients at the hospital. Some had been shot down during reconnaissance flights over enemy territory. Others had crashed in training maneuvers; they all had had many a brush with death. Their modesty and reticence about their exploits and their fatalistic attitude toward life appealed to Amelia. At the airfield we admired the planes, especially as they came in for landing like graceful gulls, but like gulls, too, they looked awkward when grounded. Amelia would have liked to fly with our friend, Captain Spaulding, but regulations against civilian passengers were strict, so we had to be content to be merely spectators. This was Amelia's first contact with flying.

Early in November 1918, Amelia was hospitalized by a serious attack of pneumonia, so she missed participating in the wild celebration that greeted the announcement of the war's end. When she recovered sufficiently to travel, Amelia came to Northampton, Massachusetts, where I was studying in preparation for attending Smith College. Amelia stayed with me while she recuperated. We walked over the lovely country roads. When mud or slush prevented our country lane hikes, we explored the byways of Northampton. On one such walk we found a tiny pawnshop displaying a medley of dusty objects in its window. At once Amelia noticed an unusual five-string banjo, and said, "Let's find out how much that banjo costs." Amelia had a

Amelia just after her solo flight.

love for music, and had taught herself to read it easily. She had inherited from Dad the ability to play by ear, and was sure she could master the banjo fingering.

We decided that by being on "short commons" for the rest of the month we could spare the twenty-five dollars the banjo cost for "sheer foolishness." I was delighted to have Amelia show an interest in doing something "just for fun," as it was a sign she was really regaining her old *joie de vivre.* Before the week ended she had found a musician to give her lessons on the banjo, and she had also enrolled in a five-week course in automobile mechanics. The incongruity of the two activities did not strike her because she was always so: artistic and impractical on one hand and scientific and intensely practical on the other.

 At the end of the summer of 1919 Amelia enrolled as a pre-medical student at Columbia University, New York, and I began my freshman year at Smith College in Northampton. Amelia took two courses in chemistry, organic and inorganic, also two biology courses, one of which she took in the university extension program, meeting evenings and Saturdays. "For fun" she audited a course in French poetry.

Amelia's closest friend during those days was Louise de Schweintz, who was preparing for admission to Johns Hopkins medical school. One afternoon as the two climbed the steps to the impressive Columbia library, Amelia glanced up at the dome, remarking, "Wouldn't it be fun to climb up there and look out over the city?"

A few days later Amelia managed to talk the library's custodian into telling her where the key was hidden which opened to the door leading to the narrow stairway from which a trap door opened onto the base of the dome. Late that afternoon, after finishing at the laboratory, the girls found the key, climbed the spiral staircase, and with all their strength pushed open the trap door and stepped out onto the narrow walkway at the base of the dome. They walked slowly around the dome, identifying Amsterdam Avenue and the Cathedral of St. John the Divine. Broadway stretched straight downtown as far as one could see in another direction. One-hundred-twenty-fifth Street and the misty Hudson were to the north.

As they sat overlooking the city, with their feet propped on the railing, they talked about their future. Louise was trying to decide whether to marry the man who wanted her to do so instead of going to medical school. Amelia suggested she should ask him to wait two years. "I don't think you should give up your career, while he goes on with his."

Louise nodded as she said with a little smile, "You know, what I think I'm really afraid of is that no one else will ever ask me. More than half of my class in college are married and most of them have babies already. Suppose after two years Bert doesn't ask me again. I'd hate never to have a family of my own."

"I can think of lots of things worse than never getting married," declared Amelia vehemently, "and one of the worst is being married to a man who tied you down. I'm not sold on marriage at all for myself, but, of course, I'm not in love with anybody—yet."

Professor James MacGregor recognized and appreciated the work Amelia and Louise were doing in his biology course. He and his assistant frequently invited them to have tea in their office after the afternoon laboratory period. In order that the invitation should not be obvious to the other students, the professor would leave a small piece of paper torn in the shape of a T on their laboratory desks. They would be purposely slow about cleaning up after the period, and as soon as all the others had left, would join the men to enjoy a cup of tea brewed in a beaker over a Bunsen burner. Here they discussed informally the significant experiments being carried on at Columbia and elsewhere "in the greatest of all sciences, biology."

Dr. MacGregor said of Amelia later, "She grasped the significance of an experiment, mentally assayed the results, and drew conclusions while I was still lecturing about setting up

Shellacking the canvas wings on Snooky's plane.

the experimental machinery. She was a most stimulating student, and when she and Louise de Schweintz worked together they were a remarkable team. I feel that had Amelia not become caught up in the adventure of flying, she would have found equally challenging frontiers to conquer in the laboratory."

At the end of that year Amelia went to California, where our parents were living in Los Angeles. Dad was working as a lawyer, and with the help of a local member of the Christian Science Church, had got the better of his liquor problem. About the time Amelia arrived in California, he was admitted to the Christian Science Church. His Church friends further helped him by bringing legal business to him occasionally, so by the summer of 1921, Dad was again established as a fairly prosperous and respected member of the community.

Because the pleasant house in which our family lived on Fourth Street in Los Angeles had more space than they needed, Mother agreed to rent two large rooms to three young men who had been sharing a suite at the Y.M.C.A. Amelia's letters to me at Smith contained more and more mention of one of these, a young chemical engineer named Samuel Chapman, a graduate of Tufts University from Marblehead, Massachusetts. The quiet, well-read New Englander was attracted to her, too, for they enjoyed tennis and swimming, as well as discussing books and plays. They had a common interest in "the underdog," and, although traditionally and logically on the side of property and order, they were interested in the socialist doctrine exemplified by the still virulent Industrial Workers of the World.

Amelia staunchly upheld her ideas of fair play especially in regard to the rights of those less fortunate. Later, we who knew her well would not be surprised at her choosing a career of social work, where she would be making a tangible contribution to the welfare of "the other half."

Early in the spring of 1920 Amelia had written to me at college that she was interested in taking flying lessons. Remembering her disappointment at being forbidden to fly with the Royal Flying Corps officers in Toronto, I was not surprised. She was working in a telephone office to earn money to pay for her lessons. She wrote me, "I want you to meet my instructor, Neta Snook, 'Snooky' to everybody on the field. She dresses and talks like a man and can do everything around  a plane that a man can do. I'm lucky that she'll teach me, not only because she will give me lessons on credit, but because she is a top-notch flier and one of the first women to get a pilot's license in Canada."

When I came West early in June I was eager to learn more of this hobby of Amelia's. I went out to the airfield with her. Snooky, her face smirched with daubs of grease and her tousled hair windblown, greeted me with engaging frankness. "I hear you're a college gal. Well, if you've got a quarter the flying sense of your sister, you'll do all right without more college." She won my heart by her unstinted praise of Amelia who, she declared, was a "natural." Standing with Snooky, I watched Amelia solo about a week later. We gathered around to congratulate her as she climbed out of the plane. She took the teasing in good part, but then she said, "It's so breathtakingly beautiful up there, I want to fly whenever I can!"

The chances to fly did not come so very often in those days of pioneering. It was a hand-to-mouth existence for the group of pilots gathered at the airfield where Frank Hawks took brave souls aloft for ten minutes for a dollar. They were like any Bohemians, dedicated to their art and united in scorning the one-foot-on-the-ground multitude who, for their part, regarded all pilots as slightly crazy. On Sunday mornings, Amelia and I used to bring out to the airfield a market basket with sandwiches and a chocolate cake that mother was always willing to bake for us. The temperature on the field was often above one hundred degrees and the

The neighborhood children loved the low-slung model car.

powdered adobe soil rose like a cloud whenever a plane took off or landed, for the paved runway was still in the distant future. There were some tin-roofed shacks for tools and gasoline, but no hangars. I often shellacked the canvas wings on Snooky's plane for her or replaced rusted guide wires. If there had been few paying passengers, the pilots saved their gasoline and, sitting in the shade of the shed, let their imaginations soar, since their planes could not.

After becoming a pilot Amelia wanted a plane of her own. She managed to raise the money to buy a small used Kinner Canary biplane for her twenty-fifth birthday, July 24, 1922. In this plane she set a new altitude record for women by flying to 14,000 feet. The record only lasted a few weeks, but Amelia enjoyed the flying.

Between my junior and senior years at Smith, my family decided to invest the last of my mother's family legacy in a mining venture, in the hope of building the money up again to a substantial sum. But, just as the mine was beginning to succeed, a flash flood filled the quarry. Without expensive pumping equipment, work could not be resumed. Our investment was lost.

Shortly after this Dad and Mother decided on a divorce, and our family was split. I wanted to return to the East to work for my A.B. degree. I came to Boston, and got a teaching job in a suburb, Medford. Amelia sold her biplane and bought a yellow Kissel sports car, in which she drove Mother east to join me. Sam Chapman, happy at the disposal of the plane, soon followed Amelia East, and her life seemed destined to fall into a conventional and pleasant pattern.

Amelia also looked for a teaching job. At a venture she answered an advertisement in a Boston paper asking for a part-time teacher of English to the foreign-born at Denison House, a neighborhood house in Boston's Syrian and Chinese Harrison Avenue district. She was interviewed by Miss Marion Perkins, the head worker of Denison House. In spite of her lack of formal social work experience, Miss Perkins engaged her at once.

Miss Perkins early appraised her as a potential leader. It was obvious to her, as it was to Mother and me, that Amelia had found a consuming vocation. She took a personal satisfaction in helping her pupils (many of them twice her age) over the language hurdles and watching them attain greater self-confidence day by day. Given free rein, Amelia entered into the work with boundless enthusiasm visiting, teaching, comforting, and loving many of the families of her neighborhood. Amelia often drove her yellow Kissel car with several teenage girls to our home in West Medford for picnics in the yard or for storytelling and marshmallow roasts around the living room fireplace. The neighborhood children loved the low-slung sport model car, which was called affectionately the Yellow Peril. Frequently she let as many as ten children climb in or stand on the running-boards while she drove slowly around the block. For many of them it was their first ride in an automobile, so they used to beg her to drive past their homes where they could wave to their families gathered on the steps or sidewalks.

The *Friendship* takes off from Boston Harbor.

Soon Amelia was a full-time worker living at Denison House. Her work annoyed Sam Chapman, who wanted her to marry him. The more Sam urged her to be married, the more she shied away, clinging to her freedom. Sam, mistakenly imagining that Amelia objected to his irregular hours as an engineer for the Boston Edison Company, once declared, "Meely, I'll be whatever you want me to be. I will get other work tomorrow if you say so."

Far from being impressed by his eagerness to please her, Amelia was annoyed. Later she said to me, "I don't want to tell Sam what he should do. He ought to *know* what makes him happiest, and then do it, no matter what other people say. I know what I want to do, and I expect to do it, married or single!" Sam also expected Amelia to stop working if she married him, and the thought of "living the life of a domestic robot" was impossible for Amelia. But refusing to marry him was a difficult decision for her to make.

When Amelia came to Boston, she kept up her flying. She demonstrated Kinner planes for prospective customers, and was allowed the use of one when no customer was around. In the spring of 1927, Mrs. Frederick Guest, another woman pilot, who lived in England, had bought a Fokker trimotor plane in which she hoped to cross the Atlantic. When she yielded to her family's opposition, she wanted another woman pilot to replace her as a goodwill ambassador between America and England. Amelia was asked.

The telephone call came while Amelia was at Denison House rehearsing her students in a play. She resented the interruption, so her reply to the polite query, "Miss Earhart?", of Mrs. Guest's agent, Captain Railey, was a brusque and hasty, "Yes, this is Miss Earhart. What do you want, please?"

Captain Railey came to the point with true soldierly directness: "Miss Earhart, would you be willing to do something important for the cause of aviation—such as flying a plane across the Atlantic?"

Amelia's impatient foot-tapping ceased abruptly; details seemed unimportant; her decision was immediate. "Yes," she said, simply. "How could I refuse such a shining adventure?" She took a leave of absence from her job.

After Amelia was approved by Mrs. Guest's representatives in New York, among whom the principal was the New York publisher George Palmer Putnam, she was given a legal contract for the flight. All expenses involving the plane and personnel were to be paid by Mrs. Guest. Amelia was named captain: her decisions, once they were airborne, were to be final. She was to serve without pay, and any income from royalties or advertising contracts, "consistent with the dignity and integrity of the sponsor and the undersigned," should be turned back towards the flight's expenses.

Commander Richard Byrd, the Arctic explorer, was made technical consultant for the flight. He selected as pilots to fly with Amelia Wilmer Stultz and Louis Gower, and as mechanic "Slim" Gordon. Their plane was christened *Friendship*.

To avoid publicity Amelia never saw the plane until the day of their takeoff. Everyone became tense as bad weather reports delayed their flight. They feared a rival would forestall them. Amelia made her will and wrote farewell letters to Mother and Dad—just in case.

Early in the morning on June 4, 1927, five men and Amelia met in conspiratorial silence. They stopped at an all-night lunch counter, and had the thermos bottles filled with coffee for the men and cocoa for Amelia, and bought sandwiches. When they reached T Wharf Amelia, Bill, Lou Gower and Slim climbed aboard the tugboat *Sadie Rose* and chugged through the wispy mist to the anchored orange Fokker. Slim, balanced on the pontoons, expertly spun the props. Bill soon had the motors racing, while Slim, after casting off from their mooring, swung

Amelia printed a message, weighted it with two oranges and as Bill circled over the deck, dropped it.

into the cockpit beside Bill. Amelia leaned across the two oil drums behind them. Lou Gower, crouched at the extreme end of the cabin, hoped to help bring the nose of the plane up by his added weight there. Twice the ship was gunned across the harbor, but it did not lift. A five-gallon tank of gasoline was jettisoned, but to no avail. Lou Gower's one hundred sixty-eight pounds might make the difference, so Bill taxied back to the float, where Putnam and Railey were waiting, and Lou jumped out. The next time across the harbor the *Friendship* responded, the pontons slanted upward, and they were airborne!

"Eureka!" sang Amelia

"At last!" grunted Bill.

"I'll have a sandwich!" said Slim.

The shining adventure had begun.

Quickly the newspapers picked up the story, and besieged Mother and me for interviews and pictures. Meanwhile the *Friendship* had landed in Newfoundland to refuel, and was delayed there by thick fog, day after day. Amelia sent a telegram to Mother, saying, "Know you will understand why I could not tell plans of flight. Don't worry. No matter what happens it will have been worth the trying. Love, A." Mother had me send back this message: "We are not worrying. Wish I were with you. Good luck and cheerio. Love, Mother."

In Newfoundland, day followed dreary day as the plane tossed hopelessly stormbound in the tiny harbor. The newspapers criticized the fliers for their seeming reluctance to take to the air again. Finally a favorable weather report on June 12 sent the fliers out to the plane with high hopes. Bill tried every angle across the bay to get the distance to lift the plane from the grasp of the water, but to no avail. The salt water spray seeped into the motors, making them sputter and lose power just when it was most needed. It seemed as if all nonessential equipment had been discarded in Boston, but now even a camera and blankets were taken ashore by the discouraged trio. On two succeeding days again they tried in vain for a takeoff. The plane must be lightened still more, so after another heart-breaking failure to get into the air, Amelia agreed to unload nearly three hundred pounds of fuel. She realized, as the men did, that this was lowering the safety factor, but in a desperate situation, desperate measures were necessary.

Under pressure of the tension, pilot Stultz sought relief in drinking. The impetus of the adventure was gone and he could not face the thought of ridicule and failure. He drank compulsively, doggedly, until he reached the state where he did not need to think. Amelia and Slim worked in every way to keep him from drinking. Finally, after fourteen days, they got a favorable weather report. The sun was shining for the first time since the *Friendship* had anchored in the harbor, as Amelia pounded on the men's door on the morning of June seventeenth. When Slim opened the door, he gestured despondently toward the snoring figure.

Cold water on the outside and hot coffee inside eventually enabled Bill to get to his feet. Steadying him between them, Amelia and Slim went down the steep path to the wharf. Amelia arranged with the local storekeeper to send the code word "Violet" to Putnam in Boston, one-half hour after he saw the plane lift from the water. A small group of friendly villagers gathered at the waterside as word spread that the fliers were going to "try again." The sun's shining seemed propitious, and many spoke encouragingly and wished them luck as they embarked for the plane's mooring in the little dinghy.

It was nearly eleven o'clock when they climbed aboard the plane, cast off, and Slim spun the propellors to start the motors. A sullen Bill gunned the motors, and hardly giving Slim time to slip into the copilot's seat, began recklessly to taxi across the bay. He swung the ship into the wind at the last moment before the *Friendship* piled up on the rocky breakwater. To lift the plane from the water a speed of from fifty to fifty-five miles per hour was required. Amelia, leaning over the oil drums behind the pilot's seat, saw the speed indicator creep up to forty-five and then fall back as Bill had to swerve to avoid heading into the open ocean. Bill turned and looked questioningly over his shoulder at Amelia.

Suddenly a blessed break in the fogbank revealed —land!

"That was so near, Bill," she said. "Do try it once more and I'll push even harder from back here."

With a nod of agreement Bill headed across the bay, adroitly swung the plane around at the farthest point again and roared for the open sea. The water was thrown out like spreading wings on each side; the whole plane was vibrating violently; Amelia closed her eyes as she saw the speedometer tremble at fifty. In a second or two more the *Friendship* was again a creature of the airways.

Bill's hand on the throttle was steady, but his face was mottled, and he was feverish and cross. Had she done right to entrust their lives to him? Well, the die was cast, worrying now would be futile. Slim announced happily that he had radio contact with Halifax and a coastwise excursion steamer. Bill throttled the engine to cruising speed as he set the course east by south at approximately 2500 feet altitude. Amelia turned to the improvised chart table to begin writing the log. She had just made the entry, "Trepassey Harbor, June 17. Airborne at 11:40 A.M." when she caught sight of a whiskey bottle, three-fourths full, tucked between the ribs of the fuselage and the small bag of Slim's essential tools. It was Bill's, of course. Amelia was in a quandry. Her first impulse was to open the hatch a crack and drop it into the Atlantic. Suppose Bill demanded a drink, and there was none to give him? The consequences might be disastrous. She decided to leave Bill's liquor where she found it and hope he would not come looking for it.

About three hundred miles offshore, they encountered a bank of fog. Bill, trying to escape the fog by reaching for higher altitude, nosed into a freak snowstorm. Even fog was less to be feared than ice on the wings, so, without warning, Bill nosed down at roller coaster speed that sent Amelia sliding against the oil drums back of the pilot's seat. He levelled off at a lower altitude, but the driving rain and headwinds slowed them for more than a hundred miles until they outran the squall and emerged into a belt of clear sunlight over a sparkling ocean. The motors were singing in symphony as the plane winged its way on course. Bill turned the controls over to Slim, eased down in his seat, and in two minutes was asleep. Amelia, kneeling by the chart table, noted in the log the change in pilots. Two hours later at about seven o'clock, she wrote: "Seven hours out of Trepassey. The greatest sight is the sun splashing into oblivion, showing pink through apertures of the distant fog. I wish the sun would stay longer. We shall soon be gray-sheathed."

An hour later Bill again took the controls, and Slim stretched out on the floor of the fuselage. Amelia wrote: "View too vast, too lovely for words. Light of our exhausts is beginning to show as pink as the last glow in the sky. I am kneeling here by the chart table, gulping in beauty Radio contact *Rexmore*, Britisher bound for New York."

At ten o'clock she scribbled: "Darkness complete. Bill sits alone, every muscle and nerve alert. Slim sleeps. There are many hours to go."

At midnight she waked Slim, who ate a tremendous Trepassey salmon sandwich, and four chocolate bars. Then, after helping Bill take a star fix, Slim again slipped into the copilot's seat and Bill dozed a little, while Amelia curled up on the floor and slept until about four o'clock. She was wakened by hearing Slim working with the radio, calling for any ship hearing them to "come in." No answer was forthcoming. The *Friendship* was alone, a speck over a vast empty ocean. They had been in the air more than sixteen hours; now there was an estimated four, possibly five, hours of fuel left. They should be near some part of the British Isles, but without radio contact they had to depend on Bill's navigational skill alone. Dawn came, but in Amelia's log there is no mention of the beauty of the sunrise; the struggle for survival was pressing too hard upon her consciousness. All three searched the endless gray waters when Bill came through the clouds. Again and again they were certain they saw land, only to have it disappear, a tantalizing mirage. At about half-past six they sighted a ship, later identified as the S.S. *America.* Hoping to get a bearing, Amelia printed a message, weighted it with two oranges and, as Bill circled over the deck, dropped it. She missed the target, and they did not dare use their

The *Friendship* is finally welcomed to Burryport, Wales.

fuel to circle again, for now they were using their emergency tank and had less than an hour's supply left.

Rain and fog added to their plight. Suddenly a blessed break in the fogbank revealed a cluster of factory chimneys less than a mile offshore, and the three, sighting it simultaneously, sang out the mariners' ageless paean, "Land!" in chorus. Although Amelia knew they were not at Southampton, any port spelled success to the bone-weary crew. Bill dropped down onto the smooth water of a small bay and Amelia dutifully recorded the fact: "20 hrs. 40 mins. out of Trepassey *Friendship* down safely in harbor of _____." The blank was not to be filled in for nearly an hour while the fliers rocked in the plane in a torrential downpour.

The landing at Burryport, Wales, partook of a comedy scene. Amelia waved and called to longshoremen at work on the quay. They waved back perfunctorily and continued the work of the day: loading a British lighter with fine Welsh coal. Eventually, just as Bill threatened to taxi the plane against the pier, a small boat put out from shore. The single occupant was a harbor policeman.

As he approached the plane a look of amazement crossed his face. However, a stout Welshman, secure in his knowledge of the correct performance of his duty, was not to be daunted by the unexpected sight of a woman in trousers who had unceremoniously anchored an orange plane in his harbor.

"Do ye be wantin' something?" he asked, touching his streaming sou'wester with two fingers, in deference to Amelia's sex.

"We've come from America," she said. "Where are we? What place is this?"

"Have ye now?" the representative of law and order asked in a slightly patronizing tone. "Well, I'm sure we wish ye welcome to Burryport, Wales. I'll go see about getting ye mooring space for the flying machine, and getting ye ashore."

In less than a half hour, Amelia saw a large launch carrying several easily recognizable town dignitaries and a cameraman leave the wharf. Bill was helping Slim put the tarpaulin covers over the motors. His back was towards Amelia. She quietly picked up the whiskey bottle which had worried her so much twenty-two hours and two thousand miles ago and thankfully dropped it into the water. Bill had not touched it or even asked about it during the gruelling flight.

The fliers had to undergo a reception before getting what they wanted most—warm food and a chance to sleep. Captain Railey arrived to greet them: he had crossed the Atlantic by steamship while they were held up in Newfoundland. When he praised Amelia for having made the trip, exhausted and overwrought, she jerked away from him, saying almost fiercely, "I was utterly useless. Those two, Bill and Slim, could have done it alone. I was just a sack of potatoes!"

Throughout the publicity and receptions that followed, Amelia continued to insist that the real hero of the flight was Bill Stultz, the pilot-navigator. She felt unhappy about receiving the lion's share of the applause because she knew that her contribution to the actual flight was practically nil. Again and again she called herself a sack of potatoes, a backseat driver, a deadhead passenger.

During her time in London Amelia managed to find a chance to visit Toynbee Hall, and see how British social workers coped with the problems she had seen in Boston. She also got a chance to go flying with Lady Mary Heath, Britain's foremost woman pilot, and ended up buying her small Avion plane and bringing it back to America with her on the ship.

When Amelia returned to the United States, she was received as a heroine, with parades in New York, Boston, and Chicago. George Palmer Putnam had a contract with her for her to write a book for his firm about the flight. She stayed with the Putnams in Rye, New York to write the book, which she called *20 Hrs., 40 Min.*, the time the flight had taken and the final entry in the logbook. After finishing, she decided to fly across the United States in the new Avion plane she had bought in England. Her trip was full of adventures—all flying was at that time. There

The plane turned over, the propellor cracked and splintered, and Amelia hung upside down, held by her safety belt.

were few aids to the flier, who had no instruments to guide him when he could not see, no radio to lead him to the next airfield, and whose airplane could not always be trusted to perform as it should.

Amelia made few preparations for her cross-country flight. Fliers in those days used road maps to guide them in flying over land. If one was lost, he looked for a river or a railway line, and followed it, hoping it would take him to a town before he ran out of fuel. When one found a town, one tried to guess what it could be. Some of the few air-minded towns painted their names on top of a large roof in the town, to aid the bewildered pilot.

Amelia had a number of problems on her flight, many of them typical of the state of aviation at that time. When she came to land at Rogers Field in Pittsburgh, her first stop, she found it was, like most airfields at that time, a field, with grass growing in it. She flew over once, looking to see if there were rocks, holes, ditches, or other hazards. She came around, aiming at landing on what looked like the smoothest part of the field. As the plane came in, one wheel hit a shallow ditch hidden by grass. The plane turned over, the propellor cracked and splintered, and Amelia hung upside down, held by her safety belt. She turned the motor off, and managed to get out, unhurt.

Another plane had to be flown in from New York, so that parts from it could be used to repair hers. Four mechanics worked around the clock a day and a half to fix her plane. Then she was ready to take off again.

After more flying, she found herself in Texas. Flying in bumpy weather, aiming at El Paso, Amelia found that her roadmap kept sliding from her lap to the floor. She found a safety pin in her handbag, and pinned the map to her dress. But when her regular gastank, which fed gasoline to the engines by gravity, was nearly empty, Amelia had to reach up to pump fuel from the reserve tank into the regular tank. The pin loosened from her dress, and when a gust of wind blew into the cockpit, the map went over the side. She was now flying with no guide but common sense.

She kept heading the same way she had been going. Finally she crossed a highway, and turned to follow it. When it suddenly ended, she had nothing. The sun was beginning to set, and soon it would be too dark to land. She had to find a place to land quickly.

She came to a small town, but could see no place nearby which looked likely for a safe landing. Suddenly an idea occurred to her. The main street was long and wide, and there was no traffic. She landed successfully on the dirt Main Street of what she discovered was Hobbs, New Mexico. Climbing out, she commandeered some of the local men to help her fold the wings of her plane, and park it off to the side of the street, before she settled in for dinner at the Owl Café.

When she started her takeoff the next day, her left tire blew out. The local men repaired it, but when she landed again, back in Texas, it went flat. She was lucky that the plane did not turn over. After the tire was repaired again, Amelia, fresh from luncheon with the local Rotary Club, started off again, still trying to get to El Paso. This time, as she was flying at 4,000 feet, she had engine trouble. The engine began making unhappy sounds, coughed, sputtered, and stopped. This sort of thing often happened to early airplanes, and early pilots quickly grew expert at looking for the best place to land when they had to land somewhere quickly. Amelia found a small clearing among mesquite bushes and salt hills, and successfully glided into it.

She was near a road: cars stopped, and their passengers came running to help. The plane was finally towed back to Pecos behind a car. It took three days for the necessary engine parts to reach Pecos from El Paso, 187 miles away, and for the engine to be repaired. Then Amelia was off again, for the West Coast.

She landed successfully on the dirt Main Street of what she discovered was Hobbs, New Mexico.

On her return flight, she had one more emergency landing without engine, ending up in a plowed field in Utah. Her plane nosed over, but she escaped unhurt. She went on. That was the way flying was in those days.

After finishing her book Amelia gave a series of lectures, and wrote articles for *Cosmopolitan* magazine. She was a celebrity, getting two hundred letters a day. There were requests for autographs from schoolchildren, some kindly letters of praise and appreciation, a scattering of "crank" letters, including offers of marriage, begging letters, and, of course, a few vituperative letters. She was asked to send a check for one hundred fifty dollars to pay for a woman to obtain a divorce because, she wrote, "I know you believe in women's freedom." The morning after she had lectured before a women's club in Westchester County, Amelia received a letter asking her to send the writer the dress she had worn. "I am just about your size and I know you will not wear an evening dress twice. I will be waiting eagerly for it." The children's letters Amelia tried conscientiously to answer, although requests for autographs were granted, as Amelia said, "by squiggling my name" on a form postal card.

Amelia bought a Lockheed plane which was larger than her Avion, so she could enter the Women's Air Derby to be flown from Santa Monica, California to Cleveland, Ohio. This race marked a milestone for women in aviation. For the first time in formal competition women were recognized as pilots capable of long flights without direction from men. Amelia, although she was undoubtedly the best-known entrant, placed only third, but winning was immaterial to her. The important consideration to her and to all the other fliers was the fact that in more than two thousand woman-hours of flying, covering three days, there was not a single serious mishap, and only two emergency landings, both of which were safely negotiated.

Amelia was one of the pilots who organized a club for women pilots, called after the number of its members, "The Ninety-Nines." She was chosen the first president, and served from 1929 to 1933.

She took a cross-country flight in an experimental autogiro (a forerunner of today's helicopter) sponsored by the Beechnut Packing Company. En route she set two new records. With her profits she sent Mother to see England, a long-time dream of hers. This was only one of the many generous ways in which she used the money she now had at her disposal.

Amelia about to depart on her transatlantic flight.

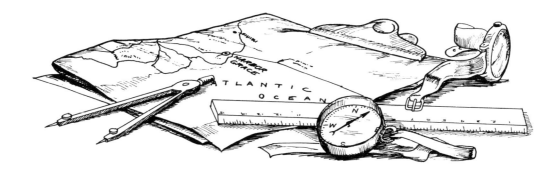

In February 1931 Amelia married George Palmer Putnam, her publisher. GP, as he was known, declared that he had proposed to Amelia six times, the last time being in the Lockheed hangar while she was waiting for her plane to warm up. Amelia simply nodded her head, then patted his arm and climbed quickly aboard.

Amelia was reluctant to take on the responsibilities of marriage, and feared that marriage might interfere with her accomplishing the things she wanted to do. On the morning she married GP she handed him a note putting down in writing her view of what their marriage would have to be.

> *Dear GP;*
>
> *There are some things which should be writ before we are married. Things we have talked over before—most of them.*
>
> *You must know again my reluctance to marry, my feeling that I shatter thereby chances in work which mean so much to me. I feel the move just now as foolish as anything I could do. I know there may be compensations, but have no heart to look ahead.*
>
> *In our life together I shall not hold you to any medieval code of faithfulness to me, nor shall I consider myself bound to you similarly. If we can be honest I think the difficulties which arise may best be avoided. . .*
>
> *Please let us not interfere with the other's work or play, nor let the world see our private joys or disagreements. In this connection I may have to keep some place where I can go to be myself now and then, for I cannot guarantee to endure at all times the confinements of even an attractive cage.*
>
> *I must exact a cruel promise, and that is that you will let me go in a year if we find no happiness together.*
>
> *I will try to do my best in every way . . .*
>
> *AE*

Their marriage worked well. They had an intelligent and affectionate comradeship which weathered many unusual stresses. GP acted as a sort of business manager for Amelia.

Knowing Amelia's desire to advance aviation, GP was not surprised when she remarked one April morning in 1932, over the breakfast buttermilk, "Would you mind if I flew across the Atlantic alone this spring?" Within a matter of minutes GP had arranged a meeting with Bernt Balchen, a skilled Norwegian flier, who, they decided, was the man to mastermind this flight.

The following eight weeks were filled with rigorous conditioning of Amelia and her Lockheed Vega. Eddie Gorski, an expert Lockheed mechanic, was recruited by Bernt. In order to avoid the publicity which would hamper her training regimen, she chartered her plane to Bernt, who was known to be considering an antarctic flight. Amelia had flown the red and gold Vega for nearly three years, so there was nothing unusual in having all ailerons replaced and a new engine and auxiliary fuel tanks installed, presumably for Mr. Balchen's Polar journey. Several new instruments now decorated the instrument panel: a drift indicator, two compasses, and a directional gyrocompass. For this flight, as Amelia had declared four years before, there were to be no pontoons.

At about eleven o'clock the plane was hit by a heavy squall.

"I'll just have to keep going until I get to land," she said, half jokingly, to GP. "You know I hate to get my hair wet."

Once again, the moment of starting depended on the weather reports. The go-ahead came May 19, while Amelia was with her plane at Teterboro Airport.

Amelia drove as rapidly as she dared back to Rye. She slipped into tan jodhpurs, white silk shirt, and a mannish windbreaker whose plainness she relieved by tying a gay blue and brown scarf around her neck. She tucked a toothbrush and a comb in a case and put it in her pocket. Stopping in the kitchen, she told the housekeeper not to prepare dinner for them that evening. Her flying suit was already folded under the copilot's seat in the Vega, and she knew two cans of juice were in the map rack. There was nothing else she planned to carry on her trip to Europe. At the airport, GP gave her a folded twenty-dollar bill with the husbandly advice to telephone him as soon as she landed.

That night Bernt and Eddie flew the plane to Harbor Grace, Newfoundland, while Amelia slept on the floor of the plane. After having her thermos bottle filled with hot tomato soup, Amelia went towards her plane, which Bernt was warming up on the runway.

A fringe of sycamore trees cast long shadows in the early evening. The fragrance of spring was in the air, as Amelia looked from the greening fields to the rocky shores and the restless waves beyond. Had anyone asked her why she wanted to risk her life alone over the seemingly limitless expanse of water, I imagine she would have said with a shrug and a smile, "Why, for the fun of it, of course!"

In her heart she would have admitted that the real reason for this flight was to wipe out the stigma she felt at being only a passenger on the *Friendship*. Amelia, however, was thoroughly convinced that safe flying was important for the United States and the world; hence, each flight had to open an exciting frontier which eventually would become commonplace.

After shaking hands with Bernt and Eddie, Amelia climbed into the pilot's seat. Leaning out of the cockpit window, she shouted above the motor's roar, "Thank you both, again, and good-bye!"

"Skoal, Amalie!" called Bernt, using the Norwegian version of her name, as he held both arms aloft in a victory salute.

Amelia was airborne soon after seven o'clock on the evening of May 20. Within an hour, she was engaged in a duel for life between the elements and the Vega. Ice formed on the wings as she sought altitude to avoid the swirling fog which was covering the water. She set a course due east, flying as near the surface of the water as she dared to keep the wings free from the treacherous slush. At about eleven o'clock the plane was hit by a heavy squall, and as Amelia glanced at the altimeter, she was appalled to see the dials spinning around and around. Somehow during the buffeting of the storm, the delicate adjustment of the instrument had been disturbed, so now Amelia was like a ship without a sounding lead sailing among hidden reefs. The clouds that had obscured the moon were suddenly blown away and Amelia saw the heaving seas not more than seventy-five feet below—a pretty narrow margin of safety. Amelia blessed Bernt for insisting that she have a gyrocompass installed in the plane, for now she saw that her speed indicator was as inaccurate as her altimeter, and that she must navigate solely by the tiny needle and ball.

Amelia set the weary Vega down in James Gallagher's pasture on the outskirts of Londonderry.

At some time past midnight, she became aware of an added menace: from a broken weld in the manifold ring of the motor exhaust, flames were streaming. It was not immediately dangerous, but if the other sections became loosened by the engine's vibrations, the motor might explode because the fumes could not escape. Amelia faced the terror of death in a burning plane. She had passed the point of no return.

All her skill was needed to keep the plane on course. Icy wings alternated with dangerously low altitudes. The high rolling waves seemed almost to reach for her when she dived through the cold mists to free the wings of ice. As dawn came, the storm lessened in intensity, but Amelia knew she was using borrowed time with the flaming manifold. Ocean flying just before sunrise is often tantalizing and dangerous because of the occasional occurrence of mirages. As happened in the *Friendship* flight, Amelia "saw" land three times before her true landfall of the Irish coast. Peering over the side of the the cockpit to try to gain an inkling of her location, she spotted some railroad tracks which she proceeded to follow until she was over a fair-sized city. Alas! There was no airport visible. She dared not risk more time in the air, so, banking sharply, she flew back a few miles to circle above a farm which she had noted had a smooth expanse of grazing land, not too thickly dotted by cows. Amelia set the weary Vega down in James Gallagher's pasture on the outskirts of Londonderry, Ireland, approximately fifteen hours after taking to the air at Harbor Grace.

Amelia used her twenty-dollar bill to cable GP. As soon as he heard of her safe arrival he rushed from his New York office where he had spent the night, mentally flying with her. He reached the North River Pier just in time to get aboard the S. S. *Olympic*, sailing for France.

Amelia was received with enthusiasm in England, then joined GP in France. The French Senate had voted to receive her, the first woman of a foreign country to be invited within those sacred precincts. She was awarded the Cross of the Legion of Honor by the French minister, M. Painlevé, who, five years before, had similarly decorated Colonel Lindbergh. She received other honors at the same time from other European governments. When Amelia returned to the United States, President Hoover presented her with the National Geographic Society's gold medal for her contribution to the science of aviation. Congress gave her the Distinguished Flying Cross.

In the years from 1932 to 1936, Amelia flew hundreds of miles and logged several thousand flight hours in her Lockheed. She made a nonstop transcontinental speed record for women pilots from Los Angeles to New Jersey; the following year she shaved her own record by approximately two hours. In 1934 Amelia made preparations to fly from Hawaii to Oakland, a flight no one had yet made successfully.

On Christmas Day in 1934 Amelia and GP boarded the S.S. *Lurline* bound for Honolulu, with the Lockheed Vega securely lashed on the forward deck. They were accompanied by Paul Mantz, a well-known pilot who had been Amelia's technical advisor for her transcontinental flights. After many delays and difficulties, she took off from a muddy field in a downpour. The takeoff of a heavily loaded plane is hazardous even with a smooth dry field, but when the plane's landing wheels sink into two or three inches of sticky mud, the danger is doubled. Amelia's Lockheed, loaded with five hundred gallons of gasoline, the radio equipment, and the other extras weighed more than three tons. Added to the difficulty of a "slow track," Amelia had no wind to help her lift the ship; the whole strain would have to come on the engines. Paul Mantz had placed white guide flags along the runway with two checkered flags marking the spot where she must brake the ground speed and return if she had failed to be airborne. An Army ambulance, marked with a large Red

Making an emergency landing on a dried lake bed in Mexico.

Cross, and a detachment of twenty men each with a portable fire extinguisher lined the runway.

Amelia laughed at the ominous precautions. "It surely looks as if they didn't expect me to make it, doesn't it, GP?" she said as she climbed into the cockpit. "Watch me fool them!"

She gunned the motors; slowly the ship began to roll. As it approached the dreaded checkered flags, the motors seemed to be delivering every ounce of power possible, but it was not enough—then the plane hit a small ridge and bounced upward as Amelia pushed the throttle full ahead. She was airborne with just twelve feet to spare.

Compared with the takeoff and the Atlantic crossing, this flight was uneventful. After eighteen hours in the air, she arrived at the Oakland Airport, where ten thousand people were waiting to welcome her.

Within three months, Amelia took off on two "Good Will" flights to and from Mexico City—one from Los Angeles, California to Mexico, and the other from Mexico to Jersey City. On the first flight, she got lost, and had to make an emergency landing about fifty miles from Mexico City. She found what looked like a pasture, but was in fact the bed of a dried-up lake. Although she could not speak Spanish, and the crowd of Mexicans who gathered about her plane could not speak English, she managed to get them to show her the direction to Mexico City, and help her take off. Half an hour later, she was in Mexico City.

She enjoyed seeing Mexico, especially when GP joined her there. He helped her solve the problem of taking off for her flight to New Jersey. Mexico City is 8,000 feet above sea level. At that high altitude, a plane needs longer to take off. Amelia's plane would be heavily laden with gasoline, which would mean that even more space was required. The military airfield, Mexico City's flying field, had a runway shorter than she needed.

GP arranged to clear the dry bed of Lake Texoco of obstructions, so that three miles of runway were available for her. She then waited eight days for favorable weather reports, loaded her plane with 470 gallons of gasoline, and ordered one hard-boiled egg and one sandwich to take along. The plane took off with only one mile of runway. Flying over the beautiful

mountains which surround Mexico City, Amelia was on her way. She crossed the Gulf of Mexico, and flew up the east coast to Newark, where a huge crowd of people waited to welcome her.

When Amelia returned from Mexico, President Edward Elliot of Purdue University in Lafayette, Indiana, heard her participate in a panel discussion on "Women and the Changing World." After listening to her defend the younger generation's right to experiment, Dr. Elliot decided he wanted her as a visiting counsellor for the women students at Purdue. She was to provide a model and offer advice for girls who wanted a career. At first she planned to be on campus one week out of every four, but soon she found that she had enough to do there to keep her at Purdue three weeks out of four. She and the students liked each other, and Purdue interested her as the only university in the country with its own airport as part of its department of aeronautics.

At Purdue Amelia lived in one of the women's dormitories. She talked with the girls about possible careers. "I'm inclined to say that, if you want to try a certain job, try it. Then if you find something on the morrow that looks better, make a change. And if you should find that you are the first *woman* to feel an urge in that direction—what does it matter? Feel it and act on it just the same. It may turn out to be fun. And to me fun is the indispensable part of work."

At Purdue University, Amelia was a visiting career counselor for women students.

Amelia always insisted that one of the best reasons to do anything was because you wanted to. When people criticized her because she explained that the motive for her Atlantic flights had been that she *wanted to*, she answered, "It isn't, I think, a reason to be apologized for by man or woman. It is the most honest motive for the majority of mankind's achievements. To want in one's own heart to do a thing for its own sake; to enjoy doing it; to concentrate all one's energies upon it—that is not only the surest guarantee of its success, it is also being true to oneself."

The trustees of Purdue University decided to establish a fund for aeronautical research, and one of the uses to which this fund was put was the purchase of one of the newest Lockheed planes, an Electra. To Amelia's surprise, this plane was turned over to her. She quickly realized that now she had a plane with which she could take up the challenge of flying all the way around the world, and began making her preparations for such a flight.

Nearly a year's preparations were required. Amelia and GP had to make sure that fuel and supplies would be waiting at each planned stopping point, and that all the countries Amelia would visit were ready to receive her. When she revealed her plans to reporters, they asked, "Why are you making this flight, Miss Earhart?"

Her reply was, "I hope this flight will yield some valuable knowledge about human reactions and mechanical performance at high altitudes and high temperatures for long intervals. I am racing nobody, but I do have a time schedule which I shall endeavor to follow. I am not interested in setting any records; I hope the data we shall bring back on fuel consumption and other mechanical details, as well as airport facilities and conditions, may hasten and encourage worldwide civilian plane travel. The flight has been carefully plotted to cover the maximum distance with the minimum number of stops."

Amelia thought of this as her last long flight. It began March 17, 1937, when she and her crew left Oakland, California, for Hawaii. With her were Captain Harry Manning of the U.S. navy, her navigator, Fred Noonan, a veteran Pan American Airways pilot and navigator, and Paul Mantz, friend, pilot, and technical advisor.

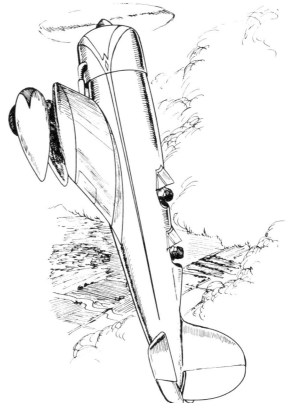

In Hawaii on March 19, the Electra warmed up to take off for the long hop across the Pacific to tiny Howland Island, its next stopping point. As the heavily loaded plane tried to take off, something failed. One wing was practically sheared off as the plane veered out of control. Amelia's instant reaction in cutting off the ignition prevented the plane from becoming a funeral pyre for the fliers trapped inside. Thankfully unhurt, the three wriggled out of the canted plane while the fire apparatus poured sand and chemicals on the gasoline leaking from the punctured wing tank.

GP in Oakland sent a radiogram, "So long as you and the boys are okay the rest doesn't matter. After all, it's just one of those things. Whether you want to call it a day or to keep going is equally jake with me."

Reporters crowded around the fliers as they sadly made their way toward the hangar. They clamored for the answer to one question, "Will you give up the flight now?" Amelia, characteristically squaring her slim shoulders, said firmly, "Of course not! I shall certainly try again."

A spontaneous cheer broke from the small crowd—a tribute to an unquenchable spirit.

One wing was practically sheared off as the plane veered out of control.

The Electra was brought back to the California Lockheed factory for repair. Meanwhile Amelia and GP replanned the trip. New money had to be raised to pay for the expensive repairs. Weather conditions suggested that Amelia would do better to fly east around the world, instead of the originally planned west. When the money had been raised, Amelia wired President Elliot, "Future is mortgaged, but what else are futures for?"

By the time the plane was repaired, Captain Manning had to return to duty. Fred Noonan took over as navigator. On June 1 Fred and Amelia set out from Miami, Florida, sending back dispatches to be sold to the newspapers. Amelia kept careful records of the Lockheed's performance and of the reactions of Fred and herself to climatic changes, altitude, fatigue, and diet. First they flew to South America, then crossed the South Atlantic Ocean to Africa, where Amelia was charmed by the Morroccan bazaars.

From Dakar, they flew on across the African continent. Flying over desert was as dangerous as flying over ocean: in both cases there were no landmarks for guidance. They flew to Gao, on the upper Niger River, where their fuel awaited them. From Gao they went to Fort-Lamy beyond Lake Chad, where they saw an occasional hippopotamus. The heat was over 100° when they landed. They flew on to El Fasher, then to Khartoum in the Sudan.

From Khartoum they went to Massaua in Eritrea, crossing a tall mountain range en route. The temperature there was often over 120°. They had reached the Red Sea.

As they had been refused permission to stop in, or even fly over, Arabia, Amelia and Fred flew down the Red Sea to Aden, then flew along the southern Arabian coast, then across the Gulf of Oman to their landing point, Karachi—then a part of British India, now part of Pakistan. In Karachi Fred and Amelia took the opportunity to have a ride on a camel.

As they crossed India to Calcutta, large black eagles dive-bombed their plane. They also found themselves involved in the monsoon season, the period of storms coming off the Indian Ocean. Difficult flying lay ahead, with storms in the air, and muddy airfields on the ground.

From Calcutta they pushed ahead to Akyab, where they hit a storm so severe that they had to turn back. She determined to fly over the storm to Bangkok, Thailand, but when they stopped to refuel in Rangoon, Burma, another rainstorm caught them.

On the morning of June 20, they went on to Bangkok, refuelled there, and headed on to Singapore across the Gulf of Siam.

June 22 they left for Java, one of the Indonesian islands. While their plane was being serviced and checked for the difficult flying ahead, Amelia and Fred drove up to look into one of the Javan volcanoes.

They went on to Bandung, discovering en route that some of their navigation instruments were not working. On June 27 they left Bandung, hoping to reach Australia, but had to land after five hours on the island of Timor. From Timor they flew on to Port Darwin, Australia, and on June 30 from Port Darwin to Lae, New Guinea.

Ahead lay the most dangerous and longest leg of their flight—2500 miles to tiny Howland Island in the Pacific. It was a small target, with no alternate landing points nearby. The Coast Guard cutter *Itasca* was anchored off the island to broadcast radio signals as an aid to the flyers, and to hunt for them if they encountered problems. It was a long flight, and, if anything went wrong, the danger was great.

Vicious head winds and rain squalls, the forerunners of the dreaded monsoons, kept the plane grounded for twenty-four hours. On the morning of July first, Amelia and Fred climbed aboard, checked their instruments, signaled, "Ready!" and waved to the crowd which never failed to gather to watch the great plane take to the air or come in for a landing. The Electra, although heavily loaded, was airborne well before the end of the runway, which terminated in a cliff overhanging the water. Three hours later Amelia radioed back to Lae, giving her position as eight hundred miles over the Pacific, directly on course for Howland Island.

In Dakar, Amelia bought some peanuts in the market.

During the night and in the early dawn of July second, Amelia's radio signal was heard by the Coast Guard Cutter *Itasca*, but there was too much static for communication to be established. Amelia reported a heavy overcast and asked for her position, but evidently she could not receive the directions sent out methodically by the Coast Guard personnel under Commander Warner K. Thompson. The fruitless efforts of the *Itasca* to establish satisfactory radio contact with Amelia concluded at 8:45 on the morning of July second when she gave an incomplete bearing of "155-337, running north and south." Utter radio silence for three hours led the *Itasca* commander to send out the message that Amelia was presumed down in the ocean with a dead transmitter.

From Washington, D.C., Admiral William D. Leahy started the machinery for a Naval search of approximately two hundred twenty thousand square miles of ocean. With emphatic support by President Franklin D. Roosevelt, Admiral Leahy ordered the *Lexington*, the Navy's largest aircraft carrier, several destroyers, and other available craft stationed on the west coast to crisscross the area south and east of Howland Island. Literally thousands of tiny atolls were visited by the ships or scanned from low-flying planes sent out from the great carrier. After fifteen days of exhaustive search, the Navy sadly admitted defeat. As the *Lexington* steamed through the Golden Gate, she briefly lowered her colors to half staff in tribute to two gallant American fliers who had made their last flight.

Further searches were made, fruitlessly. Various rumors about the fate of Amelia and Fred developed from time to time. Some suggested that they had become prisoners of the Japanese government. But no evidence supported any particular theory.

We like to have our mysteries solved; I wish I could satisfy all of us by producing an unimpeachable solution. That I cannot do, and, at this point, I believe no one can. In concurrence with many who sail the beautiful and fickle Pacific and who now fly over her waters, I agree with Commander Thompson's theory that Amelia's plane was submerged within seconds after her last radio message and within a hundred miles of Howland Island. The Electra, shattered by the impact with the high seas, sank with her passengers trapped in the twisted cockpit. In a deep abyss of the ocean's floor, the wreck will lie, a hostage of the sea, until one of the world's nuclear submarines may someday resurrect it.

A reporter for the *Navy Times* suggested that valuable experience was gained from the search, and that procedures for future emergencies were worked out. "Gradually the mistakes of this flight and the search have become the basis of improved techniques that have saved many lives since then and are still evolving more effective measures. Miss Earhart flew to advance the interests of aviation. That was her mission. She may not have accomplished what she set out to do in this last flight, but advance aviation she did."

The manner of Amelia's death is not of great moment to me now. That she did not live to have a child of her own and to enjoy the honors she had earned is sad. She escaped what she dreaded, the advancing years, demanding that she relinquish her vital activities and inevitably bow to physical disabilities. Amelia loved life each day from the time she slid down the slippery homemade roller coaster as a pig-tailed bundle of energy to the day in July, 1937, when she climbed aboard her beloved Electra in Lae, well knowing the hazards, but resolutely facing the odds and playing for greater stakes than ever before. I say, "It was fun having you as a sister, Meely!"

When his brother was killed in battle, the Roman poet Catullus travelled far to the east to visit his grave. He ends the poem he wrote there with a final greeting and a final farewell to his beloved brother: *"Ave atque vale!"*—"Hail and farewell!"

Utter radio silence for three hours led the *Itasca* commander to send out the message that Amelia was presumed down in the ocean with a dead transmitter.